Letters to Grief

Kristen Thomason

Presentation by *BookLeaf Publishing*

Web: www.bookleafpub.com

E-mail: info@bookleafpub.com

ISBN: 9789360948740

First edition 2024

The First Baby

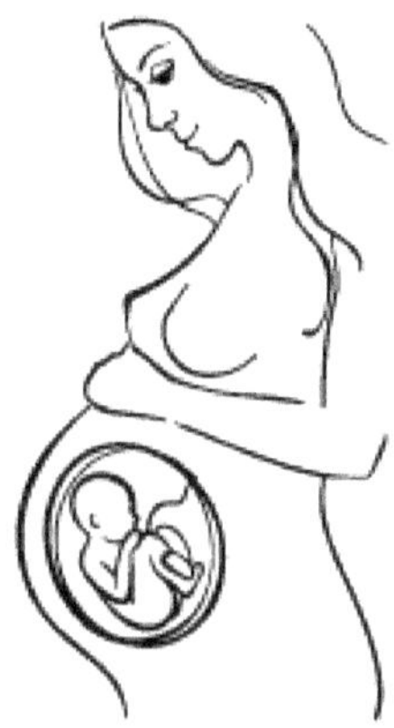

The little pink line was all we needed
To fill our hearts with bliss
What fear we all had, as we pleaded
To not have a baby that we all missed

Every twinge, every spot of blood
Caused our hearts to stop, our world to freeze
And threaten to bring our world down with a
thud
But everyone told us we just had to believe

A sneeze, a gush of blood caused us to weep one
day
As we thought our baby was lost
So away to the hospital we went without delay
We didn't even stop to count the cost

"Your baby is fine", the young doctor said
Our beautiful baby was still there
So no more tears were shed
And the pregnancy continued with prayer

You Never Came Home

You never came home one night
And it wasn't because we had a fight
When they told me you were in a car crash
Suddenly my world lay in ash

When I went to the hospital, there you were
But I wasn't so sure
You looked nothing like my husband did
So in the bathroom I hid

When I came back, I took a closer look at you
The doctor said he would be in the room in a
few
Your skin was as white as a sheet
Except your arm and face which did bleed

"No chance….he's gone," the doctor explained
So I stood there and proclaimed
That I would take care of our son, he would be
fine
I was his mother by God's design

So instead of coming home that night
You became our donor hero even in our plight

Coming Home

I came home that morning
And saw his things without warning
The fact that his socks were still on the floor
I could not ignore

His cup full of soda sat on the coffee table
And that was no fable
It sat like cement glued
And could not be moved

His clothes were still in the dryer
Leaving them abandoned prior
I took them out and held them to my face
His smell I did not want to replace

But while I held them in my hand
It did not go as planned
The clothes did not have his scent
I did not want to know what that meant

Eventually, his other clothes would lose his
scent
And increase my torment

The Funeral

It was a cold, ugly day when we laid you to rest
So when I had to get dressed
I looked like a mess
Wearing a satin black while in distress

As I shivered in the cold
I watched it unfold
They had your coffin laid out
Like a centerpiece no doubt

The mud was wet and sticky
So mom and dad got stuck pretty quickly
they missed the funeral, we all were worried
And it felt like it was hurried

I wasn't ready to leave you in the cold
But I had to go, I was told
Though I sat there as long as I could
Then I got up and there I stood

As if I expected the casket to open
And the curse to be broken
But it remained shut and quiet
So I became compliant

I wanted to see where you would be buried

So I did not tarry
But then I saw the hole and ran away
I left you there that day

It was a cold, dreary day
When I left you there to stay

I Did A Brave Thing Today

I did a brave thing today
One cold, dreary day I went to your grave
Knowing I would have to someday
In my mind, your accident I forgave

I did a brave thing today
I gently placed red roses on the nameless stone
As if I did this everyday
But this time, I thought I was forever alone

I did a brave thing today
I had to realize that I had to visit you here
And here you would forever stay
I wanted you close, always near

I continued to stand there and view
When the last time I saw the hole and ran away
But because I love you
I did a brave thing today

This Is All We Get

I took my son to see where his father lay
This is the reality
There are no family photos, no family vacations
This is all we get

I scroll through my pictures and videos
Trying to get a glimpse of our life together
Or hear his smooth, deep voice
This is all I get

I promised him I would take care of our son
There will be no kisses on the forehead by daddy
I will do my best but I know that
This is all he gets

Goodbye to Pets

I watched my pets go one by one
It could not be undone
The cats went first
But that wasn't the worst

Then went Penny, our Basset hound
I didn't want her to go to a pound
With tears streaming down
I started to drown

I could not let her go, we didn't have her long
But I knew I had to be strong
Penny went to my mother's friend
But that wasn't the end

I get pictures and texts
So that I know what happens next
Did she get a new leash or a new friend?
I never really left her in the end

I Said Goodbye to the House Today

I stood in the house for the last time today
So I wouldn't have to pay
I said goodbye to the life we had
Even though it made me sad

I stood in the doorway and cried
Not to have Adam by my side
I packed up our lives and put it away
Hoping I would see it again someday

I stood in the yard
But I didn't know it would be this hard
This is where our son should have played
What a sight that would have made!

I missed what I could not get
And I would never forget
Where the nursery should have been
And where the decals hung within

Denial

This isn't my husband at all
He'll need supper when he comes back
He'll want to call
So I'll just wait and have a snack

"Just a minor accident" I wanted the officer to
say
He might be in critical condition but people
survive
He will just have a lot of X-rays
He won't be able to drive

The doctors said "He is there"
I shook my head
Where there was supposed to be hair
There were bandages instead

Where his arm was supposed to be
There was no arm that I could see
He should look like he is sleeping that we could
agree
Instead, he looked unnaturally placed to a
certain degree

The doctors had done all sort of tests
But they just needed to do one more

I just know my husband will get up off the bed
in jest
He will not have a tube down his throat anymore

At home his cup was still on the coffee table
His computer opened, socks on the floor
Left there, as though he was unable
And after all this, I could not ignore

He wasn't coming home anymore.

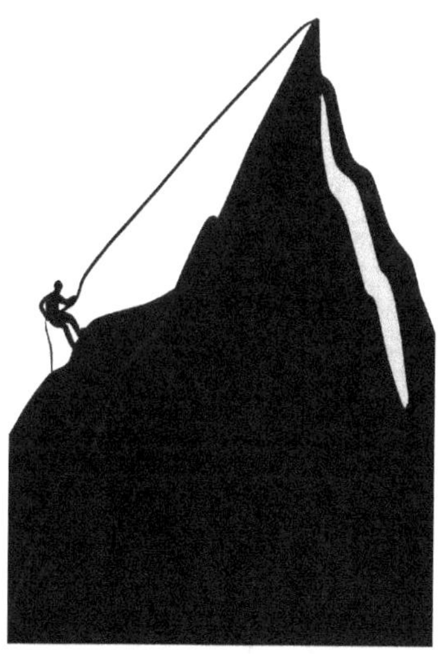

Anger

How could you leave me?
I will forever be changed
Altered
Misshapen, deformed
Broken and bitter
Was it really worth it
To pass that semi?
I am raising our son alone
Ours
How could you leave us?

Bargaining

I bargained with God
The same as you bargain for something rare
Rare as diamonds or rubies
I bargained for my husband's life
Take me
I was the one who wanted to die
Not too long ago
I wanted to leave this earth
But he took my husband instead
The one who wanted to live

Depression

I hear voices in my head
No, I don't hear them
I feel them wishing I was dead
Not knowing from where it stems

I look in the mirror expecting to see my face
My eyes were dark, my skin a ghostly pallor
I wish it was not the case
people do not know what is the matter

Lips pale as moonlight and face drawn into a
scowl
If it was cancer, everyone would understand
Instead it's not, and they think I am foul
But because of it, I can barely stand

I don't think I can get out of bed
I'm not sure I can even try
Even though it's in my head
I agree with the voices, I want to die

But I look into the next room at my son
And know that I am not done

January

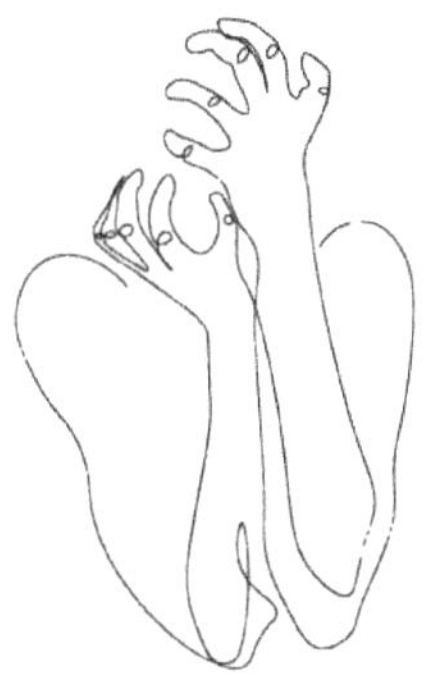

I tried to find some good in January
But I don't think I can
January is as dark as midnight
Dreary, unforgiving cold
Clutching my heart, squeezing my soul
Filled with anniversaries I do not want to
remember
January 12th was the accident which took my
husband's life
January 13th, it was official, he was gone
January 17th, they took his organs
January 20th was the funeral where we put him
in the ground
January, pitch black like coal

Deep Wound

There is a deep wound
that does not yet have a scar
I pinch it together
but the blood spills
through my fingers
down my arm
little droplets leaving a streak
drip, drip
until it pools
over time it sticks together
by itself
until all edges are knitted together

Can Anything Grow From An Ash Heap? (Acceptance)

Can anything grow from ash?
From a heap that was a life?
From tiny, gray powder that you can't count?
The ashes fall upon earth's soil and litter the
ground
With silvery snow
They need to break down and nourish the earth
Mixed with water, it is the most fertile ground
For bright flowers to bloom
out of an ash heap that was a life

The Anniversary

You died one year ago today
And all seemed dreary and gray
The rain kept pouring down
But it didn't seem to make a sound

The thoughts in my head kept swirling
And they weren't all sterling
I didn't understand why you had to go
There wasn't even snow

You were gone when you hit the wall
Less than twenty-four hours it was called
I've survived though, made it through
But I've missed you

My New Love

Life goes on, this I'm sure
Sometimes new love comes along
And blooms, love as pure
As the new blossoms that unfold after a snowy
storm
That covers the earth with a blanket of frost
Only the strongest, tallest flowers break through
the layer
Love as strong as two hearts bound together

He Holds Me Close Today

He holds me close today
because he knows it is a hard, tragic day
one year ago, they took my husband's body
his body was cut up
salvaged for parts
so that others may have a chance
my husband did not get
He may not understand
but because it is a bad day
he holds me close

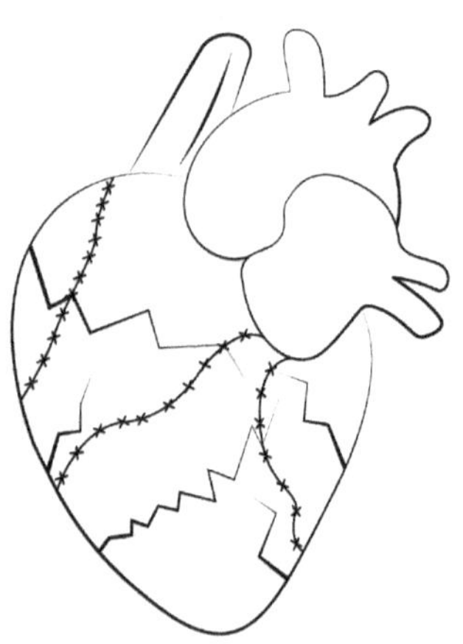

My New Life

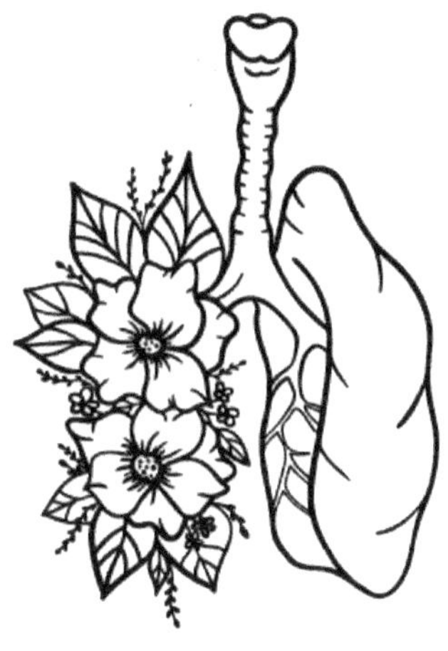

My new life isn't all that bad
yes, I lost everything and that made me sad
but I choose to look at what I gained
and that can be explained

I gained a beautiful baby
whom I thank God daily
He's bright as the sun
and new life has begun

I gained a new man
who is my biggest fan
He loves me, this I'm sure
his love is always pure

Not everything good
came from something I understood
but I can understand one thing
once again, to love I will cling

Sunrise

As bad, as black, as night can be
sunrise is always near
beautiful as it can be
peaking over the clouds
in a mixture of color
with gold, lavender, and pink hues
sunrise is always near

Toddling Baby

There is now a toddling baby
where the crawling baby once was
I wish you could have seen him
but then again, I wished you could have seen
him swim

His legs moved in perfect harmony
side to side
then taking that first step
falling once, his balance he kept

You would have been so proud
of our little boy
You would have smiled
that was just your style

But you did not see him walk
or smile or talk
He passed all these events
but your death, I can not resent

Don't Listen to Them!

I know what you might have read
About the accident and about my driving
But for your understanding, I am striving
So listen to my story instead

I was driving, maybe going faster than I should
Suddenly I came too close to a semi
anyone can panic, so don't condemn me
I felt like I needed to pass, and then decided I
would

If I had seen the second one
Then I never would have passed
I didn't know the act would be my last
I slammed on my brakes but it could not be
undone

Please believe me and trust your feelings
Would I have chosen to leave?
But I understand you need to grieve
And start your healing.

Hard Shell

There is a shell
that no one can penetrate
cold to the touch
With a soft warm center
Firm by boiling heat
Little flecks are peeled and fall
little parts that make the egg are gone

First Birthday

Today our boy turns one
In a new life full of firsts
His life has just begun
My heart, I'm sure will burst

He looks so big, so grown up
I wish I could have seen him grow
And drink from a cup
Or hear the words he knows

He no longer looks like a baby
He's more like a little boy
I think he looks like me maybe
And I hope he can someday see my joy

I love him and all that he's going to be
Although my life is over, his is not
But He must go on and see
That through him, I will never be forgotten

35th Birthday

Today would have been my 35th birthday
I had hoped you would bring flowers
And lay them on the grave for me
But I was wrong, you never came
It must be too painful to see my name on a stone

Stone

There was a mound of earth
Where a nameless stone once stood
A nameless stone that should just say birth
Instead, it said a date that could not be
understood

There was a second date that said death
But that couldn't be right
I was here, then gone with one breath
Went black as the night into the light

I was separated from my life
Like an orange and its peel
I missed my child and wife
but death can not be appealed

Once gone is gone forever
Maybe someday we will be together